A Gloucester Press Library Edition

Ancient Egypt

CONTENTS

© Aladdin Books Ltd

Designed and produced by
Aladdin Books Ltd
70 Old Compton Street
London W1

*First published in the
United States in 1985 by*
Gloucester Press
387 Park Avenue South
New York NY 10016

ISBN 0-531-17002-0

Library of Congress
Catalog Card No. 85-80642

Printed in Belgium

*Certain illustrations have previously appeared in the "Civilization Library"
series published by Gloucester Press.*

THE CIVILIZATION LIBRARY

Ancient Egypt

MIRIAM STEAD

Illustrated by
ANGUS McBRIDE, ERIC THOMAS AND JOHN BRETTONER

Consultant
C. N. REEVES

Gloucester Press
New York · Toronto · 1985

The land of Egypt

The River Nile gave rise to the land of Egypt. It starts in central Africa and flows out to the sea in the eastern Mediterranean. Each year the river overflows and deposits a layer of rich mud on the strip of land on either bank. This fertile valley is flanked by rocky desert.

Thousands of years before the birth of Christ, prehistoric hunters came from central Africa; they settled in the Nile valley and established farming communities.

Two kingdoms

Gradually two separate kingdoms emerged – Upper Egypt in the south and Lower Egypt, located in the Nile Delta, in the north. In about 3100 BC the two were united and a civilization began that was to span more than 3,000 years – longer than any since. This huge time scale contains three major periods – the Old, Middle and New Kingdoms. Egypt's famous pyramids were built during the Old and Middle Kingdoms, while the country reached the height of its power in the New Kingdom, between 1567 and 1085 BC. The last thousand years saw Egypt's decline and in 30 BC it became a province of Imperial Rome.

This time chart shows the great span of time covered by the Egyptian civilization compared to ancient Greece and Rome.

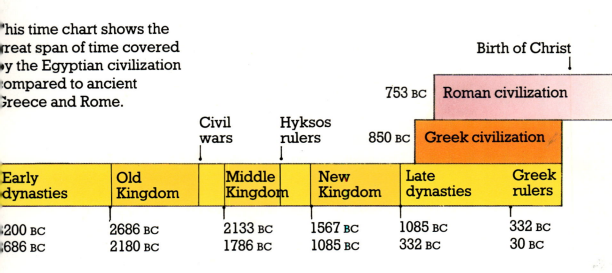

Birth of Christ
753 BC Roman civilization

| Civil wars | Hyksos rulers | 850 BC Greek civilization |

Early dynasties	Old Kingdom	Middle Kingdom	New Kingdom	Late dynasties	Greek rulers
3200 BC 3686 BC	2686 BC 2180 BC	2133 BC 1786 BC	1567 BC 1085 BC	1085 BC 332 BC	332 BC 30 BC

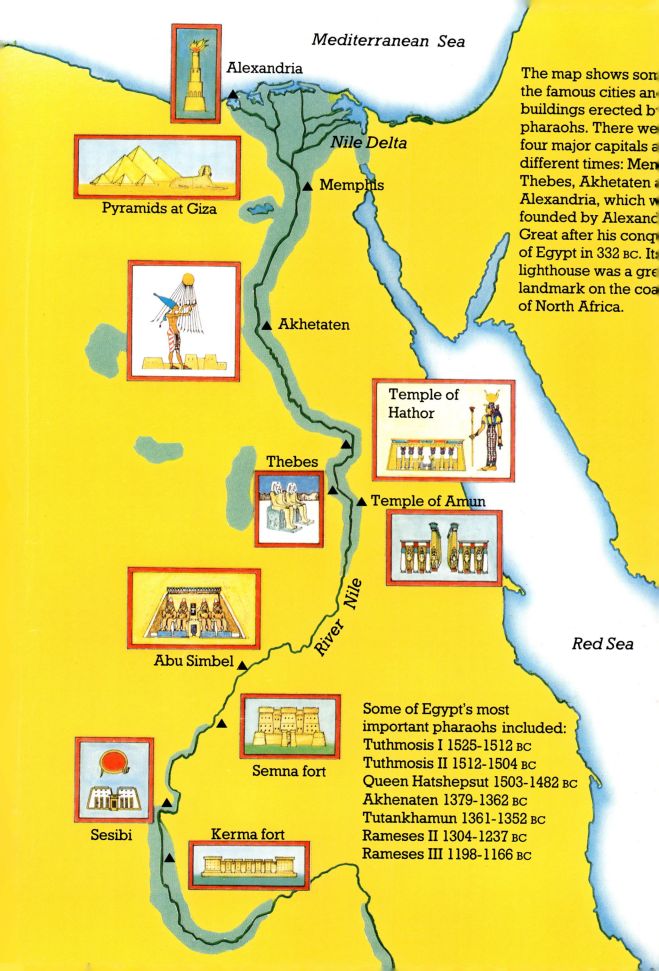

Mediterranean Sea

Alexandria ▲

Nile Delta

Memphis ▲

Pyramids at Giza

Akhetaten ▲

Temple of
Hathor

Thebes

▲ **Temple of Amun**

River Nile

Abu Simbel ▲

Red Sea

Semna fort

Sesibi

Kerma fort

The map shows som
the famous cities an
buildings erected b
pharaohs. There we
four major capitals a
different times: Men
Thebes, Akhetaten a
Alexandria, which w
founded by Alexan
Great after his conq
of Egypt in 332 BC. It
lighthouse was a gre
landmark on the coa
of North Africa.

Some of Egypt's most
important pharaohs included:
Tuthmosis I 1525-1512 BC
Tuthmosis II 1512-1504 BC
Queen Hatshepsut 1503-1482 BC
Akhenaten 1379-1362 BC
Tutankhamun 1361-1352 BC
Rameses II 1304-1237 BC
Rameses III 1198-1166 BC

Godlike pharaohs

Egypt was ruled by families, or "dynasties," at the head of which was the king, or pharaoh. The people thought that the pharaoh was a god – they believed that he was the son of Re, the sun god, and that when he died he became Osiris, the god of the afterlife.

As a god, the pharaoh's task was to act as a link between the gods and the people, and to control the yearly floods of the Nile. As a man, his duties were to uphold order and justice, and to protect his people from enemies.

Warrior pharaohs

Some of the greatest of pharaohs ruled during the time of the New Kingdom, when Egypt's power had spread to its widest limits. Tuthmosis I fought a campaign in Nubia and extended Egypt's frontier southward. Rameses II reigned for 60 years; for 20 years he fought wars with the Hittites, ending with a victorious battle in Syria.

One of the greatest pharaohs of the New Kingdom was a woman, Queen Hatshepsut. On the death of her husband, Tuthmosis II, she proclaimed herself pharaoh and ruled for 20 years.

The pharaohs built vast
temples to the gods –
Queen Hatshepsut's is set
among the cliffs at Deir el-
Bahri (above). Giant statues
– or "colossi" (below) –
were also put up, to
emphasize the pharaoh's
power. Many laborers
were needed to move one
of these statues.

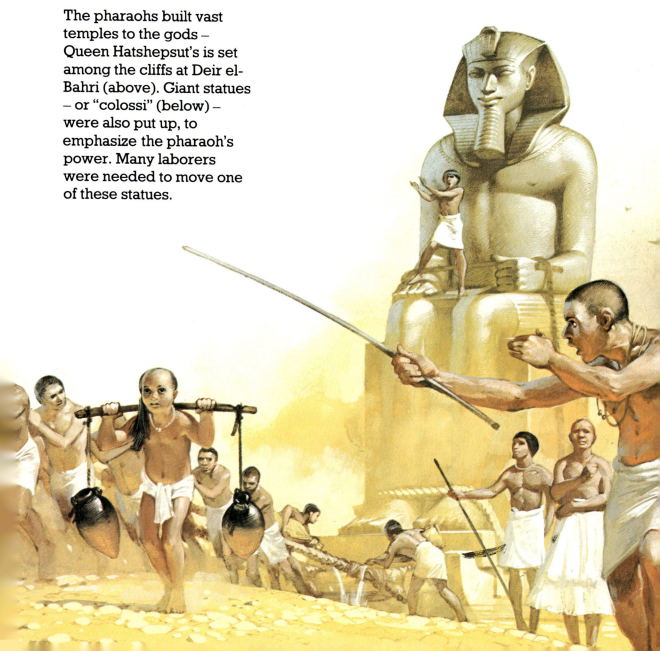

A religious people

Every aspect of Egyptian life was dominated by religion, and the Egyptians were among the most religious people of the ancient world.

Many of the Egyptian gods began as local gods, worshipped by one community. But as the country was united, some towns grew in importance and the gods of these places attracted a greater following.

Egypt had many different capital cities during its long history. At first, a city called Memphis was the capital. Ptah was god of Memphis, and so he became very important. Later, in the New Kingdom, Thebes became the capital. Amun, god of Thebes, became more and more important. He was joined with Re, the sun god, and they were worshipped as Amun Re, king of the gods.

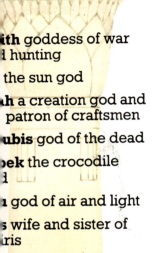

ith goddess of war
d hunting

the sun god

h a creation god and patron of craftsmen

ubis god of the dead

ek the crocodile **d**

a god of air and light

s wife and sister of **ris**

rus god of the sky

un Re king of the **ds**

djet snake god of **o**

Neith

Ptah

Re

Anubis

Horus

Amun Re

Sebek

Shu

Isis

Uadje

Horus as a child

Animal qualities

The Egyptian gods, with their animal heads and human bodies, may seem strange, even frightening, to us today. But to the Egyptians they were a familiar part of daily life. The animal aspect of the god represented qualities which were to be feared or admired.

For example, Sekhmet, the goddess of war, was part woman, part lioness, while Anubis, the god of the dead, had the head of a jackal. Thoth, the god of wisdom and inventor of writing, was either an ibis (a bird) or an ape. Hathor, with the head of a cow, was goddess of love, happiness, dance and music. Many sacred animals were also kept in the temples and worshipped – such as the cat goddess Bast at Bubastis.

Thoth god of wisd and writing

Mut a war goddes wife of Amun

Nephthys goddess women, sister of Is

Khnum the ram – a ancient creation go

Khonsu the child o Amun and Mut

Hathor goddess of and music

Osiris god of the afterlife

Sekhmet goddess war

Isis as mother god

Mut

Thoth

Hathor

Osiris

Sekhmet

Thoth

Nephthys

Khnum

Horus's sons

Isis

Khonsu

Houses of the gods

Temples were thought of as the houses of the gods and goddesses. They were built by the pharaohs, who wanted to honor the gods and who hoped to join them after death. When a new temple was built the pharaoh would give it land and great treasures; he would also add to existing temples, building shrines and statues.

The daily ritual

Priests were the only people allowed inside the temples, and every day they performed the same sacred ritual. At dawn, when the sun's rays appeared, the priests would enter and "waken" the statue of the god. They would wash it, anoint it with perfume, dress it and put out food for it. (The Egyptians, who were very practical, allowed the priests to eat the gods' food!) At night the process was reversed, and the god was put to rest in his shrine.

The people saw the gods only during the annual festivals, when their statues were carried around the countryside. Festivals were thought of as entertainment both for the people and the god, and the whole country had a holiday.

Rameses II built a great temple at Abu Simbel. It was an amazing construction: twice a year the sun's rays pierced the interior, lighting up statues of the gods deep inside.

Sun king

In the fourteenth century BC the power of the priests and the officials was thrown into turmoil by one man, the pharaoh Amenophis IV. He proclaimed that from then on there was to be one religion and only one god — Aten, the sun's disk. This new religion was centered upon the royal family, and all the other Egyptian gods were excluded. This dramatic change was very unpopular with the people.

The great temple dedicated to Amun at Karnak was closed, and another one was built, dedicated to the Aten. This temple, together with others that Amenophis built — including one at Sesibi — differed from traditional temples; the inside was open, so that the life-giving rays of the sun could stream in.

Lifelike statues of Akhenaten (right) and pictures of the sun's disk — the Aten — have been found at the site of Akhenaten's capital city, which was dominated by the Temple of the Aten (right). The sun's disk (below) is shown encircled by a serpent, an ancient Egyptian symbol of royal power.

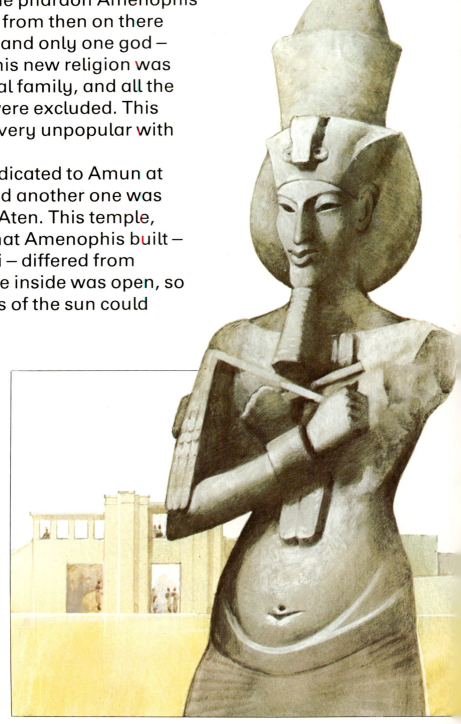

2

A new beginning

By the fifth year of his reign, Amenophis changed his name to Akhenaten and began to build a new capital called Akhetaten. Here he wished to spend his life glorifying his god. Soon a new city appeared in the desert with palaces, temples and many houses.

Akhenaten encouraged a new, realistic style of art which showed people as they really were instead of in the traditional, formal poses. Akhenaten's queen, Nefertiti, is shown as being very beautiful, but he has a pot belly and a curved spine.

After Akhenaten

Nefertiti may have shared the throne with Akhenaten for a while, and reigned on her own after his death. She was succeeded by the young pharaoh Tutankhamun; he moved the capital back to Thebes and began to dismantle the unpopular Aten cult.

Justice and the courts

The pharaoh was head of state, but he ruled through his officials. The most important official of all was the vizier, who was second only to the pharaoh. He organized taxation and maintained the system of irrigation and agriculture on which the country depended. The vizier was also responsible for the administration of justice.

The courts

The pharaoh was also regarded as the source of all justice, which was symbolized by the goddess Ma'at. Only the pharaoh could confirm a death sentence or grant mercy. The vizier would preside over major courts on the pharaoh's behalf, while in small towns and villages the mayor, or a committee of residents, would judge local crimes. Scribes would take down all proceedings in the courts. As there were no lawyers, the accused man would argue his own case, and witnesses could be beaten to make them tell the truth.

Ma'at – goddess of justice.

In this picture carved from stone, penitents kneel before the court, begging for mercy. Their crime was a common one – non-payment of taxes.

An Egyptian courtroom

Scribes

Scribes were extremely important in Egypt because they were among the few people who could read and write. The skill allowed some lowborn men to rise up in society and so enjoy the more relaxed life of the nobility.

But training to be a scribe was hard. Boys joined the scribal school at the age of five and for the next twelve years spent long hours copying pieces from classical literature, learning how to write sample letters, and writing down lists of words that government officials would need to know. The boys' education was accompanied by frequent beatings, for their teachers believed this was the way to make them learn!

Our word for paper comes from the Egyptian word papyrus. The "paper" made from it was expensive, so students practiced their hieroglyphs on flakes of stone or pieces of pottery.

Scribes sat cross-legged to write, and used a reed pen dipped in red or black ink. Below is a painted limestone statue of an Old Kingdom scribe.

An Egyptian school room

Professions

The young scribe could choose from a wide range of professions, perhaps becoming a doctor, an architect, or a clerk to a wealthy family or in a government department.

Egyptian script

The system of writing was based on the use of tiny pictures or "hieroglyphs" which represented different words or ideas. They could be written in whichever order was most pleasing to the scribe – from left to right, from right to left, or in vertical columns.

Gradually hieroglyphic script was simplified and an easier system – called "hieratic" script – was developed. Hieroglyphs were reserved for sacred inscriptions, while hieratic was used for everyday purposes.

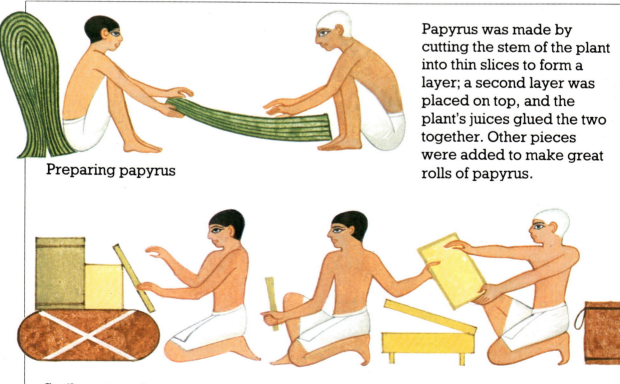

Papyrus was made by cutting the stem of the plant into thin slices to form a layer; a second layer was placed on top, and the plant's juices glued the two together. Other pieces were added to make great rolls of papyrus.

Preparing papyrus

Scribes at work

Craftsmen

Just below the administrators in social status were the craftsmen. Most of them were employed by the pharaoh, by nobles or in the temples. They labored together in organized workshops making sculpture, jewelry, furniture and many other beautiful articles. Their wages consisted of food and some clothing; sometimes they even lived in special craftsmen's villages.

First strike!

At times they went hungry — especially if funds in the royal treasury were low. In fact, the first strike in recorded history took place for this reason, when workmen at a building site near Thebes walked out because they had not been paid for two months. Chanting, "We are hungry," they did not return to work until they had received everything owed to them!

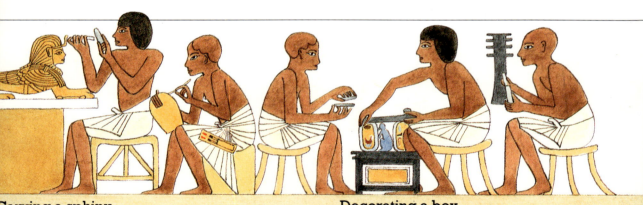

Carving a sphinx   Decorating a box

Craftsmen used simple tools of wood and bronze, such as the adz, chisel, and bow drill. There were many artists, especially in the royal tombs, where they worked in large gangs.

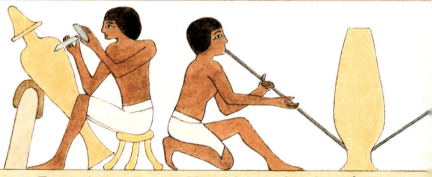

Engraving   Glass blowers heating a furnace

Workmen's villages
consisted of rows of
identical houses laid out
in a rectangular plan.

Working in wood

Weighing gold ingots

Cutting metal beads with a bow drill

Weaving

Making pottery

Life on the land

Egypt's settled way of life was based on agriculture which supplied both food and taxes. The hard-working peasants were at the bottom of the social scale, and their labor in the fields was watched over by officials who made sure that the correct amount of grain went to the government and temple granaries.

Besides seasonal work in the fields, the peasants also had the task of maintaining the vital irrigation canals. These were dug early in Egypt's history and they crisscrossed the land, allowing water to flow from the Nile into the countryside during the dry season.

The shaduf, made from a bucket and a heavy weight, raised water for irrigation.

In this Egyptian frieze, grain is sown in the rich soil; later, the crop is harvested and stacked. Honey is collected from the bees, and grapes are picked and pressed. Papyrus is cut, and geese are driven home.

Plowing and sowing

Driving domestic geese home

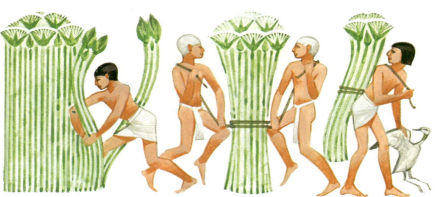

Cutting papyrus in the marshes

The farmer's year

Every summer the Nile rose, flooding the land and depositing a rich layer of silt which made it fertile. During the fall and winter, crops were sown, and in March, as the soil began to dry out, they were harvested.

The peasant farmers also kept pigs, cattle, sheep, goats and donkeys, which were used as "beasts of burden." They cut down the giant papyrus which grew in the marshes, and used it to make boats, baskets, rope and sandals. When the Nile rose again the peasants left the fields to work on the pharaoh's great building projects.

The Egyptians liked to drink milk, but also used it to make butter and cheese. Cattle were also slaughtered for meat.

Harvesting and stacking the grain

Making wine and gathering honey

Military adventures

The Egyptians were not a military people by nature. A permanent army did not exist before the Middle Kingdom, and troops were called upon only when it was necessary to defend the borders or protect expeditions.

New weapons

But in 1786 BC disaster struck. At this time Egypt was weak and divided, and so she was no match for the Hyksos people who invaded from Palestine, using horse-drawn chariots and bronze swords, which the Egyptians did not have. The Hyksos controlled the country for 200 years until the Egyptians, united once again and having learned to use the new weapons, drove them out.

Forts were set up on the frontiers – for example at Semna and Kerma. They were built of mud-brick, had massive towers and were surrounded by ditches.

A military review: Middle Kingdom soldiers were armed with bows and small axes. For defense they used wicker shields covered with animal skins.

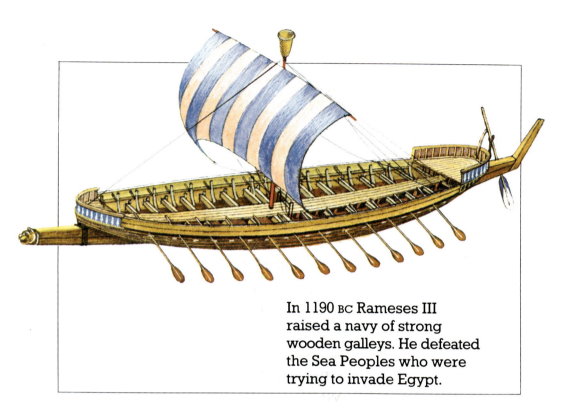

In 1190 BC Rameses III raised a navy of strong wooden galleys. He defeated the Sea Peoples who were trying to invade Egypt.

Chariots, which the Egyptians learned about from the Hyksos, were light but strong. They could turn in a small space.

Trade and tribute

The Nile was Egypt's lifeline. At the height of Egypt's power, it was like a bustling highway, carrying a huge volume of river traffic. Flimsy papyrus rafts and tiny ferries jostled with freighters loaded with cattle or grain, barges carried massive statues and slender galleys bore government officials on state business.

Trading expeditions

The Egyptians ventured onto the sea, too, and there were organized trading expeditions. They journeyed to Lebanon to buy cedar, as they had no good timber of their own. Queen Hatshepsut sent a trade expedition to the mysterious land of Punt – modern-day Somalia – and her ships came back loaded with wood, ivory and incense.

Tribute from both subject nations and allies poured into Egypt – gold and silver, copper, precious stones, scented woods, perfumed oils, horses, chariots and animal skins.

Syrian noblemen bear gifts of a falcon, an ape, golden vessels and animal skins for this pharaoh; Nubian chiefs (below) bring slaves, a giraffe and more gold.

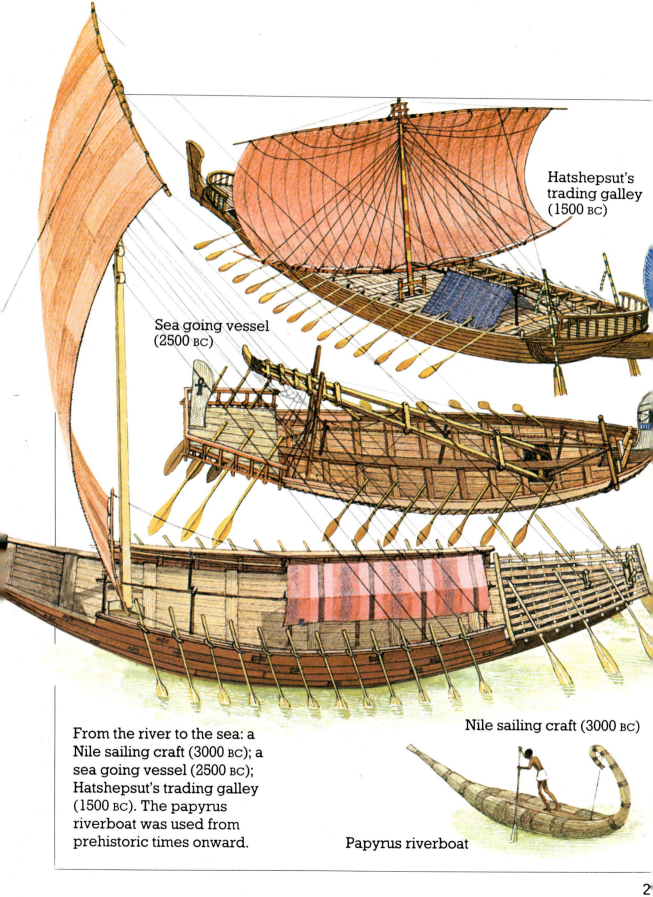

Hatshepsut's trading galley (1500 BC)

Sea going vessel (2500 BC)

From the river to the sea: a Nile sailing craft (3000 BC); a sea going vessel (2500 BC); Hatshepsut's trading galley (1500 BC). The papyrus riverboat was used from prehistoric times onward.

Nile sailing craft (3000 BC)

Papyrus riverboat

2

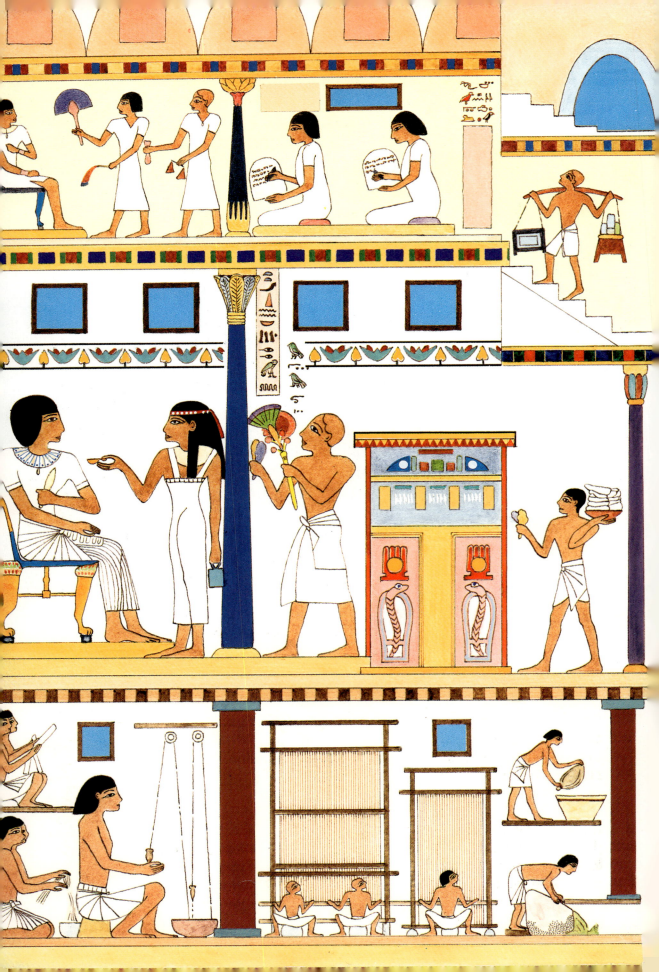

Egyptian homes

Houses were built of unbaked mud-brick with roofs made from palm branches. In the towns they were crowded together along narrow streets and were several stories high. In the country they were lower and had exotic gardens full of trees and beautiful flowers, often laid out around a pool.

Family life

Families lived in a central room which was higher and larger than the rest. In smaller houses it served as a living, dining and bedroom, but richer families would have several bedrooms and women's quarters, as well as rooms for servants. The kitchen was usually in the open, or on the roof, and contained an oven, a hot plate, a handmill for grinding wheat and bins for storing food.

Few types of furniture were used – stools and small tables were the most common. Most people had a bed, while chairs were a sign of wealth and high social status.

This picture of a house is based on a frieze found in an official's tomb. His servants bring him a meal, and he is also shown at work in his office. The kitchen is on the roof, and the servants toil up and down the stairs, loaded down with food.

Egyptian childrens' games

The afterlife

The Egyptians believed in a life after death, which they considered to be much more important than life in this world. Pharaohs and wealthy men would spend their whole lives preparing their tombs, and their bodies were preserved as mummies. Mummies were made by removing all the soft, internal organs from the dead person. The body was then embalmed in salt, washed in spiced wine and wrapped in bandages.

The quest for eternity

In the Old Kingdom only the pharaoh was thought to have an afterlife, but with the rise of the worship of Osiris, the god of the afterlife, everyone had a chance to pass to the next world. All Egyptians wished to be buried near the shrine of Osiris at Abydos.

Before entering the pleasures of eternity, the dead person had to pass a test in which his heart was weighed against Ma'at, the goddess of justice and truth. If his good deeds outweighed the bad, then Osiris would welcome the newcomer to the next world. If he failed the test, his body would be eaten by a monster which was part crocodile, part lion and part hippopotamus. The person would then cease to exist – a terrible fate to the Egyptians.

Model boats, similar to those which carried mummies across the Nile, were often placed in the dead person's tomb, to help in the journey to the next world. The mummy lies between the goddesses Isis and Nephthys, sisters of Osiris.

Anubis weighs the dead person's heart against a feather representing Ma'at.

Mummified animals

A pharaoh's funeral

When a pharaoh died he was given a magnificent funeral, after which he went to join his fellow gods. In the early days of the Old Kingdom, pharaohs were buried in mud-brick tombs called "mastabas." But between 2600 BC and 1600 BC the pharaohs embarked on a great building program, during which the pyramids were constructed. They pointed toward the sky and were believed to be the means by which the pharaohs reached the gods.

Valley of the Kings

Later, in the New Kingdom, the pharaohs and their nobles were buried in rock-cut tombs in the Valley of the Kings, near Thebes. Most of the beautiful grave goods placed in these tombs were stolen in antiquity. But one pharaoh lay undisturbed – until 1922, when archaeologists discovered the tomb of Tutankhamun.

Unloading stone for a pyramid

Building the pyramids

Gangs of peasants and craftsmen built the pyramids, probably working during the annual Nile flood. Huge amounts of stone were transported up the river on barges and then dragged up to the site.

A temple in honor of the dead pharaoh was built next to the pyramid, connected to another one on the river. The magnificent funeral ship carrying the mummy would disembark here, and the pharaoh would be laid to rest in his final home.

The Sphinx at Giza – part of the pyramid complex.

Using a ramp to raise the stone blocks

Glossary

Dynasty A ruling family is called a dynasty. 30 different dynastic families ruled Egypt during its long history.

Frieze Several of the pictures in this book are based on friezes – the wall paintings which adorn temples and tombs. They tell us much about life in Ancient Egypt. In the tombs the artists always painted the whole person because the Egyptians believed that if any part was not shown the body would be incomplete in the afterlife.

Hieroglyphs The symbols and pictures of Ancient Egyptian writing.

Hyksos people Foreign chieftains, probably from Palestine, who invaded Egypt and used new, bronze weapons.

Mastabas Rectangular mud-brick tombs which pre-dated the pyramids.

Mummy A preserved body; both humans and animals were mummified.

Sea Peoples Seaborne invaders from the Eastern Mediterranean; they were repelled by Rameses III.

Shaduf An irrigation device made from a bucket and counterweight. It transferred water from the Nile into canals.

Vizier The highest government official in Ancient Egypt; he was second only to the pharaoh.

Index